BARON

The Life of Laurence Holmes Dorcy Jr.

Kathy Lynne Linker

AuthorHouse™
1663 Liberty Drive
Bloomington, IN 47403
www.authorhouse.com
Phone: 1 (800) 839-8640

Published by AuthorHouse 01/15/2016

ISBN: 978-1-5049-6638-2 (sc)
ISBN: 978-1-5049-6641-2 (e)

authorHOUSE®

COVER PHOTO: Laurence H. Dorcy Jr. aboard the *William Crooks*, the favorite locomotive of his great grandfather, J.J. Hill (Lake Superior Railroad Museum, Duluth, Minnesota, 2010)

For Baron

…and the people who knew and loved him…

Contents

List of Images

ACKNOWLEDGEMENTS

I would like to thank all those who donated their time and energy to the creation of Baron's biography. His legacy lives on because of their vivid stories and photographs A list of the contributors can be found in the bibliography. But in particular, I want to express my gratitude to Carl Geringer for his ongoing support and input throughout the entire process. From start to finish, Carl's help was immeasurable. In addition, I want to acknowledge Jeff Peterson for his belief in this project and his positive feedback and guidance. Ultimately, I thank the Laurence H. Dorcy Hawaiian Foundation's Board of Directors for making this happen.

Foreword

I met Laurence Dorcy for the first time some twenty-five years ago in a nice San Francisco restaurant. He was not to be overlooked, fifty years old, comfortably casual, wearing a rather large Maltese cross. His introduction was "Call me Baron," perhaps referring to the WWI German pilot, Manfred von Richthofen. There just had to be a looming great story…it turned out I wasn't disappointed!

So it was with Baron Dorcy, often the most charming person in the room. There was always another improbable plan, adventure or project underway. With some combination of dreamer, military and railroad historian, and automobile collector, the vision was occasionally beyond reach - but not always. Author Kathy Linker's narrative will recount for you some of the passions and significant accomplishments of a gifted man.

By the standards of most people Baron was a very wealthy man, the fortunate beneficiary of a trust fund created by his grandfather, Louis W. Hill Sr. My career was spent at First Trust Company of Saint Paul, now US Bank, serving for many years as the administrator of L.W. Hill trusts. I had the good fortune to work with Baron, his siblings and the extended Hill family. When I retired from the bank, Baron gave me his power of attorney and asked me to help him a bit. To my surprise he also named me as the sole trustee and personal representative of his estate.

Baron died under difficult circumstances on June 2, 2011. His estate was large and very complicated. As I write this, the estate administration is near completion. Never having married, and with no children, Baron's will provided for significant, life changing bequests to thirty-five of his friends. The residue of his estate was bequeathed to thirty charitable organizations, the largest share to the Laurence H. Dorcy Hawaiian Foundation. The Foundation will ultimately be funded with about $20,000,000 and operate as a perpetual private foundation supporting Hawaiian tax-exempt organizations.

The Dorcy Foundation Board of Directors, David Barrett, Carl Geringer, John McManus, Kila DeMello, Nicklos Dudley, Isaac Hall and I encouraged Kathy Linker to write this brief biography of Laurence Dorcy. It is intended to be an introduction to a man whose legacy, through his Foundation, will serve many people in his much-loved Hawaii in future years. We hope you enjoy a good story!

Jeffrey Peterson
Trustee, Personal Representative of the Estate of Laurence H. Dorcy
North Oaks, Minnesota

Preface

The following book is a short photo biography of Laurence Holmes Dorcy Jr. It is not intended to be a full narrative of his entire life, but rather a collection of highlights based on interviews with people who knew him. A complete novel could be written about his seventy-six years of adventure on this earth. This photo memoire features only a few of Mr. Dorcy's accomplishments and escapades.

It was important to Mr. Dorcy and the Board of Directors of the Laurence H. Dorcy Hawaiian Foundation to leave behind a written record of his life. This book is a small fragment of his interesting endeavors and the abundance of stories he generated.

His name was Laurence H. Dorcy Jr., named after his father, Dr. Laurence Holmes Dorcy Sr., but he went by many names. Laurie is what his mother and childhood friends called him. Laurence was his formal name, but later he took on the nickname, "The Baron" or just "Baron". For the purposes of this book, he will be referred to as Laurence, Mr. Dorcy or Baron.

The process of interviewing, researching and writing about this wonderful man has enriched my life. He leaves behind an incredible legacy. For those who knew and loved him, his memory lives on. In addition, his generosity has supported numerous charities in Hawaii and will continue to assist many more in the future. As they say in Hawaiian, *Mahalo* Baron. Thank you.

Kathy Lynne Linker

CHAPTER ONE ~ A RICH FAMILY HERITAGE

Birthright

On January 29, 1935 in San Francisco, California, Laurence Holmes Dorcy Jr. was born into a world of privilege due to his illustrious family legacy. He was the first born of Maud Van Cortlandt Hill, granddaughter of railroad baron, James Jerome Hill, the "Empire Builder". Dorcy's great grandfather, J.J. Hill, was the ambitious Canadian-American railroad tycoon of the Great Northern Railway. The railway spanned across a significant region of the Upper Midwest, the Northern Great Plains, and the Pacific Northwest.

Although he was born in the midst of the Great Depression, Laurence grew up in an elite environment that few Americans experienced at the time. But, to fully appreciate Laurence's life, one must first understand the family ancestry of his mother, Maud Van Cortlandt Hill, and his father, Dr. Laurence Holmes Dorcy Sr.

Ancestry of Laurence's Mother ~ Maudie

On June 1, 1903, J.J. Hill's wife, Mary Theresa, wrote in her diary:

"A very beautiful day, quite cool. We are certainly blessed while so many other parts of the country are deluged with high water…. Maud and Louis have an addition to their family this evening. A daughter was born at eight thirty p.m. A healthy looking child. Our second granddaughter."

She was referring to the birth of Laurence's mother, Maud, the daughter of Louis W. Hill and Maud Van Cortlandt Taylor Hill.

The Hill family history is a very scripted tale, originating with J.J. Hill's formation of a vast railroad empire in the northern United States during the mid to late 1800s. His life was a true tale of rags to riches. His father, James Hill, was a poor Irish immigrant who worked as a farmer in Rockwood, Ontario. When he died, his son J.J. was only fourteen years old.

J.J. Hill attended Rockwood Academy for Boys on a waived tuition and worked at the local General Store to help support his mother. At the age of seventeen, he left for Kentucky to seek fortune as a fur trader. Instead, he became a bookkeeper and soon moved to Saint Paul, Minnesota where he transformed the bankrupt Saint Paul & Pacific Railroad into the highly successful Saint Paul, Minnesota & Manitoba Railway Company.

While J.J. ambitiously developed a thriving railroad empire, he continued to send money to his mother, Mary Dunbar Hill, who had remained in Rockwood. When his mother died on December 18, 1876, J.J. returned to his hometown in Canada with an impressive entourage to give his mother a proper burial. From his humble beginnings as a poor farmer's son, J.J. had forged an empire worth $63 million by the end of his life.

The *William Crooks*, a wood-burning steam engine built in 1861, was the first locomotive to run in Minnesota and handled J.J. Hill's private railroad cars (see photo of Baron, front cover). It also hauled regular passenger railcars from 1862 until 1897, before it was retired from service. After retirement, the old engine deteriorated quickly. When J.J. heard from his engineer, Albion B. Smith, that the *William Crooks* was to be scrapped, his response was, "Not as long as I live!"[1] The locomotive was restored to operation for J.J.'s 70th birthday party, and he proudly took the controls and drove it a short distance. Every year after that, until his death in 1916, he rode the *William Crooks* as part of his annual birthday celebration. Today, the *Wm. Crooks* is on display at the Lake Superior Railroad Museum in Duluth, Minnesota and is one of the few locomotives that survive from the Civil War era.

Baron's great grandfather, J.J. Hill's 74th birthday celebration (fifth from right) in front of
his favorite locomotive, the *William Crooks* in Saint Paul
(*Bain News Service*; Courtesy of James J. Hill Library, 1912)

J.J.'s second son, Louis W. Hill, Laurence's paternal grandfather, became his successor and led his railroad empire for another thirty years. He played a vital role in the creation, development and promotion of Glacier National Park in Montana, where he built several resorts. One of Louis' greatest legacies was his enthusiastic promotion of U.S. tourism and the American National Park System.

Baron's grandfather, Louis W. Hill Sr. with John Two Guns White Calf in Glacier National
Park (Louis W. Hill Papers; Courtesy of the Minnesota Historical Society, 1925)

The entire Hill family lived a very privileged life. Laurence's mother, Maud Hill, led an exceptional exciting life as a child. The family resided in the massive James J. Hill residence at 240 Summit Avenue, in Saint Paul, Minnesota, and later next door in the Louis W. Hill residence. Today, both homes still stand proud. The James J. Hill House has become part of the Minnesota Historical Society Museum, and the Louis Hill home is a private residence – meticulously maintained by its current owner.

During Maud's childhood, dignitaries visited their home often, and she traveled with her family regularly across the United States and Europe. Maud's brother, American filmmaker and artist Jerome Hill, eventually settled in southern France where he spent much of his time painting. He subsequently won an academy award for directing and producing *Albert Schweitzer*, the best documentary feature in 1957.

Laurence Jr. visited with his Uncle Jerome in Cassis, France during his European travels. Louis Hill and the entire family often vacationed in Hawaii, traveling by the only mode available at the time – ocean liners. Their trips were always first class and they stayed at the most prestigious hotel in Waikiki, the Halekulani.

Ancestry of Laurence's Father ~ Dr. Dorcy

Besides Baron's extraordinary birthright from his mother's ancestry, there was plenty of notoriety in his father's lineage, which was also Irish. Baron's great-great grandfather, Laurence D'Arcy (later changed to Dorcy) emigrated from Ireland around 1820 and opened a small tailoring business in Boston. He married Eliza Symmes, the daughter of Captain Nathaniel Holmes Downe, who fought in the Boston Navy during the American Revolution. He was also captain of a privateer in the War of 1812.

Laurence and Eliza's youngest son, John Chipman Dorcy, moved west at a young age to start a prosperous livelihood in the new frontier. He launched his career by working for Ben Holladay, known as the "Stagecoach King". Holladay ambitiously built the world's largest freight and passenger coach line, the Overland Stage from the Pony Express. Ben eventually sold his stage routes to Wells Fargo Express and formed the Oregon and California Railroad Company and the Oregon Steamship Company.

There is an interesting connection between Ben Holladay's railroad empire and J.J. Hill's Great Northern Railway. Holladay's railroad empire collapsed in 1873 and was taken over by Union Pacific. In 1897, Edward Harriman, the father of Ambassador Averell Harriman, acquired control, re-organized the Union Pacific Railroad and began the historic competition with J.J. Hill's Great Northern Railway. Thus, indirectly, Baron's great grandfathers, Ben Holladay and J.J. Hill, were connected by competitive railroad enterprises.

John C. Dorcy, in honor of his legendary employer and friend, named his first son Ben Holladay Dorcy. Nineteen years later, the families of John Dorcy and Ben Holladay were united due to the marriage of Dorcy's eldest son to Holladay's youngest daughter, Linda. Unfortunately, neither John Chipman nor Ben Holladay were alive to witness their matrimony. John died prematurely of consumption at age forty, in 1873, and Ben Holladay passed away in 1887, at the age of sixty-seven. John's son, Ben was only four years old when his father died, and by the age of seventeen, he enlisted for duty and training in the United States Cavalry.

On June 1, 1899, Lt. Ben Holladay Dorcy married Linda Holladay. The wedding announcement in the social pages of the Portland *Oregonian* described their relationship as a case of "love at first site, ripening into their engagement and happy marriage." Lt. Ben Holladay Dorcy was penned as "one of the most popular and efficient of the younger officers in the United States Army, having risen from the ranks in the regiment in which he holds his commission." Together they had four sons and the youngest was Laurence H. Dorcy Sr., Baron's father.

Baron's grandmother, Linda Holladay Dorcy with her four children in front of one of the original Overland stagecoaches; Baron's father, Laurence H. Dorcy, is peering out from behind her skirt to her right (photo taken at Buffalo Bill Cody's traveling Wild West Show in Detroit, Michigan, circa 1909)

Col. Ben Holladay Dorcy had an impressive military career. Throughout his lifetime, he served in various cavalry units, including command of a troop transport ship in the invasion of Santiago de Cuba during the Spanish-American War and performed extensive duty in the Philippine Insurrection. Due to a serious leg injury, he took a disability discharge from the cavalry and joined the U.S. Secret Service, assigned to hunting down the elusive Poncho Villa in Mexico. Just prior to his Secret Service duty, Ben served as Commandant of the Missouri Military Academy, where he enrolled all four of his sons. As World War I approached, Ben re-enlisted in the 7th Cavalry Regiment and eventually retired as a full Colonel.

Baron's grandfather, Col. Ben Holladay Dorcy & four sons; Baron's father, Laurence H. Dorcy,
is the youngest son sitting on the floor (Missouri Military Academy, circa 1913)

Col. Dorcy's youngest son, Laurence H. Dorcy, followed his father's military assignments around the country, eventually ending up at Stanford University where he played football in the late 1920s.

Parent's Marriage ~ Maud Van Cortlandt Hill & Laurence Holmes Dorcy

Maud and Laurence's romance started in the late 1920s after they met in Pebble Beach, California. At the time, Maud was living in the Pebble Beach family home and Laurence was a medical student and football player at Stanford University. After a rather long engagement, they married.

Marriage of Baron's parents, Maud Hill & Laurence H. Dorcy in Del Monte, California
(photo by *St. Paul Daily News*; Courtesy of the Minnesota Historical Society, March 16, 1933)

Their marriage, on March 16, 1933, was a formal ceremony at Saint John's Episcopal Chapel in Del Monte, California. The wedding was described in the *Saint Paul Daily Newspaper*: "Maud wore an ivory twill silk gown with a three cornered antique veil of old point De Viennese which had been worn by her mother, Mrs. Louis Hill. Instead of the customary bouquet of flowers, she carried a prayer book, which had been in the family's possession for many years. The Del Monte chapel, scene of many prominent social weddings, was decorated with branches of white fruit blossoms and countless candles. A lovely Sicilian brocade of aquamarine blue formed a background for the altar and as the bride walked to the altar, Mozart's wedding march was played by Penhas' famed string quartet." The reception was held at Pebble Beach, in the Hill family home.

Newspapers across the country reported the occasion, due to the notoriety of the bride and groom. The *Oakland Tribune* announced the wedding on March 15, 1933, and stated that Maud and Laurence "had been prominent in activities of Del Monte and Pebble Beach society."

The headline to the article in the *Daily Northwestern* read, "Heir to Millions Marries."

The *Billings Gazette* wrote, "Dorcy is the son of Mrs. Linda Holladay Dorcy of San Francisco, whose father, Ben Holladay originated and owned the famous Pony Express and was a great friend of Hill, the man who built the railroads of the northwest. Holladay also founded the California-Nevada Railroad."

The *Mason City Globe-Gazette* listed among the many prominent attendees, Maud's brothers; Louis Jr. of Saint Paul, Jerome of Paris, and Cortlandt of New York.

TIME Weekly Magazine wrote in their Milestones section, "Married. Maud, daughter of Louis Warren Hill, granddaughter of the late great Railroader James Jerome ("Jim") Hill; and Laurence Holmes Dorcy, literary grandson of Jim Hill's good friend, Pony Express Boss Ben Holladay; in Del Monte, California."

The Society pages of the *Berkeley Daily Gazette* reported, "After a month's honeymoon in Honolulu, the couple will establish their home in San Francisco."

Maud and Laurence started their marriage off with a first class cruise to Hawaii. They moved to Atherton, California where they lived a life of luxury and travel, unharmed by the depression of the thirties.

CHAPTER TWO ~ THE EARLY YEARS

Their First-born ~ Laurence Holmes Dorcy Jr.

On January 29, 1935, Maud bore her first son, Laurence Holmes Dorcy Jr. Maud and her husband hired a German governess to help care for their newborn child. A year and a half later, on June 4, 1936, they were blessed with a daughter, Sheilah. Having two young children did not impede their exciting lifestyle.

In the late summer of 1937, at the age of two, Laurence Jr. made his first voyage to Europe with his mother and father. His sister, Sheilah stayed at home with family and caregivers, as she was too young to travel. Maud packed her Louis Vuitton steamer trunk and they took a luxury liner, the *S.S. Normandie*, from the port of New York to Le Havre, France.

The *Normandie* was considered one of the greatest and most lavish ocean liners ever built. The ship took only six days to travel across the Atlantic Ocean to France. Laurence and his parents spent several weeks in Europe – sightseeing, fine dining and relaxing in style. Although little Laurie had no memory of this journey, it was his first trip to Europe!

Laurence had few memories of his childhood in Atherton but he used to tell a curious story about the German governess. According to Laurence, she would listen to the radio and shush everyone in the house by saying, "Quiet! We are listening to Das Fuehrer!" Laurence said she would sometimes make him and his sister raise their right hands to salute the Fuehrer! When the war started, she went back to Germany, and they hired a wonderful French governess, whom everyone called "Mademoiselle".

Pebble Beach, California

Sadly, his parents separated in 1939, while they were living in Atherton. The pressures of a wealthy heiress wanting to travel the world and a medical student wanting to practice medicine contributed in some part to their separation. Laurence was only four years old at the time.

Maud moved with Laurence, Sheilah and Mademoiselle to an attractive home owned by her father, Louis Hill, in Pebble Beach. Louis had purchased this large piece of land when it was still an unknown peninsula, long before the immense beauty of Monterey was discovered. It was private, undeveloped, and unpopulated. He had built a huge mansion on the property, with gorgeous landscaping and picturesque gardens. Today the area is known as Pescadero Point near Pebble Beach Golf Course on 17-mile Drive in Monterey.

Before Maud and the children moved there, the main house had burned down. But a vacation chalet remained on the property for Louis' children and grandchildren to enjoy. During her separation and eventual divorce, Maud resided in the chalet, with Laurence, Sheilah and Mademoiselle.

It was a wonderful setting for children. Laurence and his sister had a great deal of property to explore with their beloved dogs. He and his childhood friends loved to climb upon the boulders of the Rock Escarpment overlooking Carmel Bay. There were no sandy beaches, but there was tons of excitement for youngsters. There were old cars to investigate and abandoned buildings to discover – things that Laurence and his friends could do all day long.

Laurence Jr. with his mother, Maud Hill, on the beach in California
(Louis W. Hill Papers; Courtesy of the Minnesota Historical Society, 1939)

They lived in Pebble Beach for the duration of World War II. During the war, Laurence remembered that the skylights in the house were covered up for fear of potential Japanese bombers. Maud dimmed the lights at night to avoid attracting attention to the property. He also remembered some anxiety about submarines invading the area. They lost all of their Japanese gardeners during the war because the U.S. government detained people of Japanese descent.

Laurence Jr. with his sister Sheilah
at Pebble Beach (circa 1942)

Laurence Jr. at Pebble
Beach (circa 1942)

Life after the Divorce

In 1941, his parents' divorce was finalized and Maud sold their home in Atherton. Laurence Sr. graduated from Stanford University School of Medicine in 1941. As World War II unfolded, Dr. Dorcy entered the U.S. Army Air Corps as a Captain and Air Force Medic. He served with distinction in the Philippines at an air base used for launching the Tokyo bombings. He earned the Silver Star Medal for saving the crew of a B-17 that crashed after returning from a Tokyo bombing run. WWII ended and he returned to California, married his second wife, a nurse, and started a new family with her. They spent most of their time in the East Bay area. Thus, due to circumstances, Laurence Jr. had little contact with his father during his early years.

Military photo of Baron's father, Lt. Col. Laurence H. Dorcy Sr. (circa 1945)

Maud continued the lifestyle she was accustomed to. One of her passions was skiing and she loved to visit popular ski destinations. Her son, Laurence, on the other hand, despised skiing but was required to tag along on the family ski excursions. Besides disliking the sport itself, he hated the cold. He was truly destined for warmer climates.

On one of her ski trips to Yosemite, Maud met her second husband, Hannes Schroll, an Austrian alpine ski racer and Olympic champion. Hannes was a charming, charismatic, witty socialite who loved to yodel. At the time, he was the founder and owner of Sugar Bowl Ski Resort in California.

Maud and Hannes had a short engagement and were married in July 1943. They moved to a home in Woodside, with Laurence, Sheilah and the household staff. While living in Woodside, Maud bought a 640-acre property in Palo Alto, which was named Mayfield Ranch. They had a large home constructed on the lot and moved in. Horse and cattle barns were built to satisfy Hannes' passion for ranching.

Maud and Hannes had two children together, Susannah in 1944, and Christopher in 1947. Mademoiselle, who left after Laurence and Sheilah no longer required a governess, was re-hired for the new youngsters. Maud had a wing in the house built for the two boys and another wing for the two girls.

Although he was living on a ranch, young Laurence was more concerned with engine power than horses. This love affair with engines and classic cars followed him throughout his life. He admired his stepfather, Hannes, but he didn't have a lot in common with him.

However, Laurence always looked up to his biological father, Dr. Dorcy. Even though Maud remarried, it was important to her that her children maintain a relationship with their father. She once arranged a weeklong trip to Acapulco with her ex-husband and their two children, Laurence and Sheilah. Laurence was a teenager at the time and deeply appreciated the vacation with his father.

School Years

As a young boy, Laurence attended Menlo School for Boys in Atherton, California. It was a prestigious private school with a uniform dress code. He was very bright and academically years ahead of other children. He quickly advanced through grade levels, faster than other children his age.

Laurence's school photo (circa 1944)

Laurence was a gifted musician. He could pick up any musical instrument and play. As a child, he used to sit in his room at a tiny piano, with his long legs cramped underneath, and play old time rock-and-roll music like a professional. Sometimes, when he played the grand piano in the family living room, his mother would reprimand him for playing 'honky-tonk noise' rather than classical tunes.

Musical ability came naturally to him. He formally studied classical piano as a child, but quickly learned honky-tonk music on his own. The banjo, ukulele, guitar, and accordion are just some of the instruments he played without any formal training. According to a life-long family friend, he could pick up any instrument and start pounding or strumming – and it sounded great!

Throughout his youth, Laurence was a talented artist and frequently sketched his favorite things – antique cars. He also drew trains, guns and cannons. War memorabilia fascinated him. As a teenager, he started a small gun collection for target practice and collected mock battle weapons and small cannons. Comically, he often introduced himself as "Cannonball Dorcy" during his adolescent years.

He was not particularly into sports. One year, his mother built him a tennis court, which he almost never used. But he loved to swim. For Laurence, swimming was a recreational activity rather than a discipline. His homes always had lovely swimming pools, which he genuinely appreciated.

Laurence had an innate aptitude for languages. In his youth, he learned to speak first German and French, from the governesses that cared for him.

At the age of fourteen, his mother decided he needed college preparatory training before entering Stanford University, where he had already been accepted based on his academic standing. She sent him to Philips Exeter Academy in New Hampshire for a year, hoping he would complete at least two or three years before starting university. His grandfather, Louis Hill, had also attended this prestigious academy.

He was very unhappy in New Hampshire and spent less than a year there. He wanted to be back in Palo Alto with his friends. Instead, his mother recommended a year at and his grandparents' residence in Saint Paul, Minnesota. It turned out to be a wonderful stay. Although his grandfather, Louis Hill, had already passed away in 1948, Laurence thoroughly enjoyed the time he spent with William, the family's beloved chauffeur.

Louis Hill had left behind a grand collection of antique cars. Young Laurence spent most of his time in the garage learning about cars and engines. His interest in antique cars was fostered during this stay at the Louis Hill family residence.

One of Laurence's first antique cars was a gift from his grandfather. As a teenager, he loved driving his Model T Ford with its auspiciously loud engine. Later he told stories of driving this beast-of-a-car beside young ladies who rode their horses on the dirt road near his family home. He would drive slowly beside them and rev his engine until it backfired, startling the young women and their horses. It was playful innocent mischief to him, and luckily, no one was ever was hurt.

Unlike his mother, who adored an array of cultural activities, Laurence disliked plays, concerts, ballets and operas. He was expected to accompany his family on these enriching excursions. One afternoon, his family and friends were scheduled to attend a matinee play in San Francisco. Laurence conjured up a plan with a childhood buddy, and the two of them drove off in one of the family cars. When his family was ready to leave for the theatre, the two boys were nowhere to be found. His mother knew he was hiding and had her entire staff search everywhere for him. Eventually, they left for the theatre without him – which is exactly what he wanted. Afterwards, Laurence would retell this story to his friends for amusement.

While living at the Mayfield Ranch, he deepened his adoration of engines and antique cars. He would bring engine parts into his room and tinker with them for hours. Of course, his mother did not approve of her son working on greasy motors in the house – especially in his bedroom! So she had a big garage built on the property where Laurence spent countless hours working on engines and restoring old cars. His mission was to get and keep them running, usually by salvaging parts from other broken-down vehicles.

CHAPTER THREE ~ ADULTHOOD

Stanford University

In 1955, Laurence enrolled in pre-medical training at Stanford University, with hopes of becoming a doctor like his father. Unfortunately his days at Stanford were numbered due to an automobile accident that occurred during his freshman year. He required surgery and after a period of recuperation, decided to join the Air Force rather than return to college. This was another way to follow in his father's footsteps, since Laurence Sr. was an Air Force Medic who had also pursued a military career like his father before him.

Three generations of military service: Lt. Laurence H. Dorcy Jr. (left), his father, Lt. Col. Laurence H. Dorcy Sr. (right) and his grandfather, Col. Ben Holladay Dorcy in the painting (photo circa 1958)

Regardless of his short time at Stanford, he was loyal to his university and considered it his alma mater. His father, Dr. Dorcy, had studied medicine at Stanford and although Laurence Jr. did not graduate, he is mentioned along with his father in the Alumni pages – Laurence Sr., class of '38, and Laurence Jr., class of '56.

Before enlisting in the Air Force, Laurence traveled to Europe for several weeks with his father, who he worshipped. Apparently he and his father got into all kinds of innocuous mischief on the trip. After touring Europe, they met up with Maud and other family members at her brother Jerome's home in Cassis, Southern France. After a wonderful vacation with his family, Laurence Jr. reported to the Air Force.

The United States Air Force – Strategic Air Command

Photo of Lt. Laurence Dorcy on the desk in his Los Altos home (military photo, circa 1958)

After basic training, Laurence began pilot training at Reese Air Force Base, near Lubbock, Texas. He learned to fly re-fuelling tankers for Strategic Air Command (SAC). The mechanics and instruments of the aircraft, the complexities of the cockpit and the intricate flight charts intrigued him. His keen mind was like a sponge absorbing new knowledge. Flying aircraft was the most dynamic challenge that Laurence had ever faced, and he had an intuitive knack for it!

On November 8, 1957, Reese Air Force Base's newspaper, the *Roundup*, featured an article about Air Cadet Laurence Dorcy and a fellow student, James E. Ferrier. Dorcy was piloting a B-25 aircraft for his second solo flight with co-pilot, Lt. Ferrier. They were about to land the plane when they discovered a hydraulic leak. Both students carried out emergency landing procedures calmly and efficiently. Their superiors praised them for showing excellent judgment and composure in the face of danger. Dorcy kept this article in his treasured belongings for the rest of his life.

Volume VIII   Lubbock, Texas, Friday, November 8, 1957   NUMBER 51

IT BUSTED HERE!—Two students who performed outstanding work in landing a disabled B-25 show their instructors what happened. They point to the broken hydraulic line. Left is A/C Lawrence Dorcey; next is 1st Lt. James E. Ferrier. They showed great calmness and judgment. Instructors were 1st Lts. Paul Rader, second front right, and Billy J. Brown, far right.

B-25 With Hydraulic Failure Landed By Students

Newspaper article about Lt. Laurence Dorcy Jr. (Dorcy on the left; taken from the
Roundup, Lubbock Texas, Vol. VIII, No. 51, November 8, 1957)

During his Air Force duty, Lt. Dorcy became a skilled pilot of the Boeing KC-97 Stratofreighter, an aerial refueling tanker with a rigid pipe, or *flying boom*, that pumped fuel to the receiver aircraft during flight. His status as a pilot in the highly respected Strategic Air Command remained the most cherished phase in his life, and he spoke of it often. Years later, after his passing, a surprising item was discovered amongst his personal keepsakes. He had written a short poem about the importance of pilots who fly re-fueling tankers…

```
                      "TANKERS 'R US"

Awesome times in antique birds

Sounds today not often heard;

                   &          arcs
Pistons roar & prop        blurred

Those eighteen-footers really whirred!

Five flight crew feel their heartbeats stirred

Awaiting GOD's Command Post Word.


Get the flying gas pump airborn, guys--

Your bomber seeks you in the skies!

Though Terror's breath makes neck hairs rise

Takeoff! your tanker scrambles with supplies


· FOR WITHOUT US, NOBODY FLIES!

                                    Dorcy 1/P KC-97-G
```

Poem written by Lt. Laurence H. Dorcy Jr. (date unknown)

The Legends live on...

Dorcy never fought in a battle and was never stationed overseas, but he gained real life experience from his Strategic Air Command duty. He also met some honorable war heroes during his Air Force days. Lieutenant Colonel Howard Albert Bittner was one of the high-ranking military officers that he befriended. Bittner retired after thirty years of service in the United States Navy, Army and Air Force. He served on the USS *Enterprise* aircraft carrier during WWII, served in Korea and Vietnam, and flew in Strategic Air Command. He was the recipient of many medals and commendations.

Throughout his life, Dorcy remained close friends with Bittner. In 2005, he invited the colonel and a few pals on a private railcar excursion. The luxurious coaches offered sleeping accommodations for eight people and three distinct lounges, including a dining area with a full-time bartender, chef and steward. The second floor of the dining car revealed spectacular views of the western states through the glass Vista-Dome. The group traveled by rail from Chicago to Oakland over a period of a week, stopping to enjoy a distinguished boutique hotel in Denver, Colorado for a couple of nights. They also visited the Air Force Academy in Colorado Springs. This was just one of several private rail trips that Laurence arranged for himself and his friends during his later years.

Baron on a private railcar trip with Col. Bittner and others (Denver, Colorado, 2005)

Laurence often re-told the story of how fortunate Col. Bittner was during WWII. The *Enterprise* aircraft carrier, that Bittner was aboard, was scheduled to be in Pearl Harbor on December 7, 1941. Surely the ship would have been a target for Japanese bombers. However, on the morning of December 7, while still en route to Pearl Harbor, they received word that it was under attack. Immediately, the *Enterprise* launched six aircraft to retaliate against the Japanese bombers. Unfortunately they were mistaken for enemy aircraft and four were shot down by "friendly" fire.

Col. Bittner reached Pearl Harbor aboard the *Enterprise* on December 8, 1941. He never forgot the horrifying image of the harbor, still ablaze from the brutal attacks. They continued to patrol the area and sunk a Japanese submarine off the coast of Hawaii on December 10, 1941. For over sixty years, Colonel Bittner proudly carried and displayed his Pearl Harbor shore leave pass from the *Enterprise*, dated Sunday, December 7, 1941. It was a reprieve he never took, due to their fortunate late arrival.

Besides Col. Bittner, Laurence and his father, Dr. Dorcy, knew Lt. General James "Jimmy" Harold Doolittle, who planned and led the retaliatory Tokyo Raid, also known as the Doolittle Raid, on April 18, 1942. Doolittle was an incredibly accomplished aviation pioneer and earned a Medal of Honor for his valor and leadership as Lt. Colonel in the Air Force during WWII. Laurence and Doolittle continued to correspond and one of Dorcy's most-prized possessions was a photograph of his SAC unit, signed by J.H. Doolittle.

Strategic Air Command graduating class of Lt. Laurence H. Dorcy Jr.
signed by Lt. General James "Jimmy" Doolittle (circa 1958)

French Polynesia

After his Air Force days, in the early 1960s, Dorcy traveled to French Polynesia for rest and relaxation. He adored the islands of Tahiti and Moorea. Several wonderful years were spent traveling back and forth between California and French Polynesia. He stayed in Papeete and Moorea for up to six months at a time, frequenting the local bars and restaurants and appreciating the easy-going beach life.

He fell in love with the Polynesian people and the simple existence on the islands. In his travels, he met the California "Bali Hai Boys," Hugh Kelley, Jay Carlisle, and Don "Muk" McCallum and many of their friends. The Bali Hai Boys had opened the Hotel Bali Hai on the island of Moorea in 1962, and Dorcy became a frequent customer in the lounge.

On one of his many visits, he met Hugh Kelley's first Tahitian wife, Dallas Tauiari'i Cowan. When he first met her, she was a lovely young newlywed in her twenties. Today, she is still a resident of Papeete, Tahiti. Now in her eighties, she vividly recalls the day when Dorcy first saw her. According to her, he emphatically stated that she was the most beautiful woman he had ever seen in the world. And of course, he said it in perfect French!

During his time in French Polynesia, he learned some of the local Tahitian language. Moorea was very unpopulated at the time and he got to know many of the locals and other Americans who had migrated there. One of Bali Hai boys, Jay Carlisle, is still a long-time resident of Moorea. He recalled how Mr. Dorcy loved to sit at the bar and trade stories with the bartenders and patrons. Jay remembered that one of Dorcy's favorite drinks was a Starboard Light, made with crème de menthe and vodka on ice. Years later, Dorcy returned to Tahiti for his 70th birthday party, which he celebrated with American and Tahitian friends at the Hotel Kaveka.

Baron returns to Cook's Bay, Moorea for his 70th birthday (Hotel Kaveka, Moorea, French Polynesia, 2005)

Woodside Home

When Dorcy returned from his '60s era in French Polynesia, he bought his own home in Woodside, California, about a quarter mile from his mother's home.

In 1978, Ann Pettigrew, who had met Laurence years before, happened to see him at a flea market in the San Francisco Bay area. She was looking for clothes for her children and he was looking for antiques. They talked for a while about how she had recently separated from her husband and was cleaning houses for work. Dorcy needed a housecleaner, so he invited her to his Woodside home to give her a tour.

As they were walking through the house, Ann noticed a framed newspaper article on his bedroom wall that read, "In Search of a Dying Breed: The American Eccentric." She remembers thinking that he truly was eccentric, especially after she saw the car parts in his bedroom! She asked him why on earth he had a rocker arm assembly on his dresser. Dorcy thought it was remarkable that Ann even knew what a rocker arm was! He was further surprised to find out that Ann had just rebuilt her Volkswagen engine with some help from a friend.

Ann's knowledge of cars and engines helped kick-off a life-long friendship with Dorcy. He hired her on the spot to clean his house once a week, which she did for several years while living at her own apartment. Over time, Dorcy and Ann became very close friends. He had a building converted into living quarters and invited Ann and her two children to move onto the Woodside property. She also became close with his mother Maud, and his siblings, Sheilah, Suzie, and Christopher.

Laurence and his Mom ~ The Woodside Estate

In the mid 1980s, Laurence moved out of his home in Woodside and back to his mother's residence nearby. Only Maud and Mademoiselle were living in the main house at the time. Mademoiselle had become part of the family and was one of Maud's dearest friends. Maud's employees lived in separate accommodations on the property. Baron's mother often invited distinguished guests to stay on her estate. For a period of time, she even housed Russian royalty. Maud's second husband, Hannes Schroll, had moved to his own ranch, where he lived until his death in 1985.

Laurence purchased a condominium at the Colony Surf in Waikiki for his frequent visits to Honolulu. He spent most of his time between California and Hawaii. Because he was away often, he wanted to ensure that his mother received proper care. Thus, in 1988, Ann Pettigrew and another life-long family friend were hired as Maud's personal assistants.

Every night at seven o'clock, Maud would ring the dinner bell and everyone in the house would congregate for dinner. A chef always prepared the food and hired help served the family and guests. From time to time, Mademoiselle would cook her famous "Zell burgers", as the family called them. These were made from specially selected high-quality meat that Mademoiselle hand picked from the local deli.

Laurence loved to tell stories at the dinner table with his mom. Together they reminisced about childhood memories and kept the Hill family legacy alive. One of their favorite stories was about Maud's first flight with the well-known aviator, Charles Lindbergh. He was the same age as Maud and was a friend of the family. Louis Hill was very protective of his daughter. He would never let Maud go flying alone with a man. So she snuck out of the house and met young Charles, without her family knowing. When her father found out, he was livid! But Maud, attempting to calm him down, told her father not to worry. She said she would *never* go flying with Charles again since he scared her half to death with his acrobatic loops and fancy flying!

Laurence 'The Baron' Dorcy

Laurence took on the nickname of *Baron* during his Air Force days and often signed his name as Laurence 'The Baron' Dorcy. WWI German Air force pilots intrigued him. He revered the notorious Red Baron, Manfred von Richthofen, a WWI top ace fighter pilot. The nickname was also in honor of his great grandfather, the Baron of the Railroad Empire. At one point, Baron had business cards printed up with the name, *L.H. 'Baron' Dorcy*. He also wore a gold and silver Maltese cross around his neck.

Baron was an endearing and brilliant conversationalist. For him, economic status was no barrier between friendships. He had friends from all walks of life and treated people equally, regardless of their economic situation. He loved to chitchat with people, share his family heritage and show photos from the mini albums he carried in his satchel.

Baron's knapsack always contained at least one book, since he was a voracious reader. This passion began at the age of three and continued for the rest of his life. He had a curious mind and loved to read about everything. His preference was science fiction novels or historical non-fiction, specifically military, naval and air force tales. He read the entire Aubrey-Maturin series, an internationally acclaimed 20-book series of nautical fiction by Patrick O'Brien. If he had five minutes of free time, he

Laurence "Baron" Dorcy wearing the Maltese cross (date unknown)

would pull out a novel and start reading. If he wasn't chatting with people, he was reading – sometimes six books at a time!

Baron's favorite meal of the day was lunchtime. Going out for lunch was one of his main forms of entertainment. Almost every day, he would gather a few friends together to join him at one of his favorite restaurants. Because his attire was usually casual Hawaiian shirts and flip-flops, he didn't frequent restaurants with a dress code. Chinese cuisine was his preference, but he loved all types of food.

He always kept some plastic zip-lock bags in his satchel to take leftovers home with him. One can only assume that from his elite background, it was shameful to ask for a "doggy-bag" in a restaurant. He always declined the waiter's offer for a to-go box. Then, he would try to be discreet as he scooped the extra food off of his plate into plastic bags. He didn't waste food.

Baron was a kind-hearted gentleman. Once he presented the owner of his favorite Chinese restaurant in California with a pair of silver chopsticks. In Honolulu, he liked to eat at a restaurant called La Mariana Tiki Bar and Grill. Every time he ate there, he brought a flower lei to the owner, Annette La Mariana Nahinu. She and her husband founded La Mariana in 1957, and its décor is like a museum of Hawaiian memorabilia. Dorcy made a point of eating there every time he stayed in Honolulu.

One of Dorcy's close friends recalled a story of a meaningful lunch he had with Baron in 2010. Dorcy noticed an Air Force pilot, in full uniform, sitting alone at a table. He called over the waiter and paid for the pilot's lunch. Before leaving, Baron stopped at the young man's table and thanked him for his service. Dorcy mentioned he was a past pilot with Strategic Air Command and the officer shook his hand and thanked him for his service as well. Baron's appreciation for our men in uniform never waivered.

He also never lost his passion for flying aircraft. To travel between the Hawaiian Islands, he would often hire a pilot with a small plane. One such pilot, Drew Womack, said that Baron loved to fly the plane during the short flights between islands. Drew was impressed with Baron's skill and knowledge of aircraft, and the ease with which he took over the controls – especially since it had been a long time since Baron flew in Strategic Air Command.

Baron enjoys a ride in a glider (Dillingham Airfield, North Shore Oahu, 2005)

CHAPTER FOUR ~ THE HAWAIIAN CHIEFTAIN

Building a Tall Ship

While on a visit to Lahaina, Maui, Laurence Dorcy launched one of the greatest endeavors of his lifetime. He began financing and overseeing the construction of a scow schooner called the *Sea Adler*. As the project grew, and the dream and the cost ballooned, his venture evolved into the creation of a massive 103-foot gaff-rigged topsail ketch flying ten large sails. He renamed it the *Hawaiian Chieftain*, inspired by an article written by artist and historian Herb Kane about Maui's King Kahekili II.

Baron aboard the *Hawaiian Chieftain* during her construction (Lahaina, Maui, circa 1985)

At the ship's construction site on Front Street in Lahaina, Baron often socialized with the workers at the end of the day. One evening while having a beer with the boys, Carl Geringer, a ship engineer known as "Gilligan", invited him to go sailing on the weekend. Dorcy seemed a little reluctant, perhaps because he hadn't sailed for a while. But Gilligan urged him and promised him a great time on Christie Rowan's 50-foot sloop, the *R & R*. That Saturday afternoon, Baron showed up early at the dock with his sailing bag in hand, ready to go. Christie was the daughter of Dan Rowan, from *Rowan & Martin's Laugh-In*, a famous American comedy show that aired in the 1960s and '70s. Christie organized a fun crew when she heard that Baron might be sailing with them.

Due to lack of wind, they motored to Manele Bay, moored inside the harbor overnight and enjoyed the warm weather and camaraderie. The next morning, Gilligan fired up the engine for their return. Regrettably, it sputtered and died after a few minutes. Gilligan checked and discovered that no fuel was getting to the engine.

Christie was sure there was plenty of fuel so she told Gilligan to double check everything. After a meticulous inspection, and sounding the tanks, he stated again, "We're out of fuel." Baron watched intently as this scene unfolded, knowing from his own experience that the fuel tank was empty. Christie couldn't believe they were out of fuel, so she asked Gilligan to examine everything a third time.

After the third confirmation of an empty tank, Christie emphatically stated, "Gilligan! We are *NOT* out of fuel!"

Gilligan shook his head and responded sarcastically, "Okay, Christie, that's fine. We're not out of fuel. But we sure aren't going anywhere until we get some!"

Baron never forgot that humorous exchange. From then on, he and Gilligan bonded as friends. It was another one of Dorcy's favorite stories to tell. Gilligan did, in fact, borrow some fuel from a friend in Manele Harbor and the engine fired right up. They made it back to Lahaina, safe and sound. As a result of the trip, Laurence became good friends with Christie Rowan as well.

Baron & Gilligan aboard the *Hawaiian Chieftain* (Papeete, French Polynesia, April, 1990)

Launching Ceremony

As the launching day for the *Chieftain* approached, a traditional Hawaiian blessing and ceremony was planned. The ship was not complete, but it was ready to plunge into the ocean at Mala Wharf in Lahaina.

Baron's mother, Maud, who was eighty-five years old at the time, traveled from California with her personal assistant to take part in the monumental inauguration. Maud, still a lively soul, required some travel assistance, as she was elderly and walking with a cane.

Before leaving for Hawaii, an unusual thing happened to Maud at the San Francisco airport. Her aid was away for a moment, and Maud was sitting in the waiting area alone. She noticed a distinguished older gentleman sitting across from her, winking and making faces. He was an attractive white-haired man, elegantly dressed in a white suit and hat. Maud, being a proper lady, did her best to ignore his flirtations. But he continued taunting. Finally, the determined gentleman brazenly walked up to Maud and stood in front of her. Maud's eyesight was failing but before he introduced himself, she recognized who it was. It was Dr. Laurence Dorcy, her ex-husband.

Unbeknownst to Maud, Laurence had also invited his father to attend the launch of the *Chieftain*. He was eighty-three years old and had been battling cancer for quite some time. Like Maud, he needed the help of a caretaker to attend the event. Although Maud and Dr. Dorcy had not spoken for years, she was overjoyed to see him.

When they arrived in Lahaina, Maud and her assistant stayed in Baron's apartment in Lahaina on Front Street. Dr. Dorcy stayed close by and Maud decided to invite him for a special luncheon. She still remembered her ex-husband's favorite things to eat. With the help of her assistant, she arranged a shopping excursion, handpicked his favored foods and prepared an exquisite lunch for him. They enjoyed the meal together with their caretakers. Despite years of separation and the distance that had grown between them, they shared delight in their son's achievement.

On June 12, 1988, several key people were invited to the ceremony. But no one expected the entire town of Lahaina to show up! Front Street was closed, and thousands of people arrived to witness the launch of the *Chieftain*. Baron was surprised and a little nervous, but ultimately pleased by the turnout.

Laurence Jr. gave his mother the honor of christening the *Hawaiian Chieftain*. After the *Kahuna*, Hawaiian priest, bestowed his blessing on the ship and its future journeys, Maud broke a bottle of champagne across the bow with her son at her side. Maud's beaming smile expressed the pride she felt for Laurence's achievement.

With cannons blasting and thousands of spectators cheering wildly, two hefty bulldozers pulled the gigantic *Chieftain*, on its launching sled, into the water at Mala Wharf. Everyone enjoyed kalua pork from nine pigs that had been slow-roasted in the ground in traditional Hawaiian style. It was a rare event for the nautical town of Lahaina.

With the launch of the *Chieftain*, Baron gave the people of Lahaina a unique and memorable experience. Inadvertently, he also blessed his parents with a final reunion. Fifty-five years after the young couple had traveled to Hawaii for their honeymoon, Laurence and Maud were reunited on Maui for an unexpected rendezvous. They both attended the launch of the tall ship and subsequent celebrations with their first-born son. They both expressed pride at his accomplishment. Despite their age and need for caretakers, his parents traveled the distance to be there for their son's moment in the spotlight.

Less than three months later, on August 25, 1988, Dr. Laurence Dorcy died of cancer in Brentwood, California. Baron took the death of his father very hard. More conscious than ever of the impermanence of life, Laurence Jr. began contemplating the creation of his own legacy – something to be remembered by.

Baron's mother Maud christening the *Hawaiian Chieftain* (Lahaina, Maui, June 12, 1988)

The Tall Ship goes to Honolulu

On its first voyage, the *Hawaiian Chieftain* had no rigged sails and was diesel-powered. It underwent preliminary sea trials for several weeks off the coast of Maui and then motored to Honolulu and docked at Pier 40 in Honolulu Harbor. From July 1988 until January 1990, it remained at the pier for completion. Once the interior was completed and the sails were bent on, sailing trials were held and the ship became Coast Guard certified to carry forty-nine passengers.

During this time, Baron familiarized himself with his vessel. He visited Pier 40 regularly and watched the workers prepare the tall ship for the open ocean. The shipwrights, engineers, and riggers taught him, little by little, the mechanisms and workings of the boat. His clever mind quickly absorbed the new information. Baron was starting to connect intimately with his vessel. He often held social gatherings on the *Hawaiian Chieftain* to show others the evolution of his project. His excitement grew and he looked forward to the culmination of his dream.

Maiden Voyage - French Polynesia

In January 1990, Mr. Dorcy decided to ready his tall ship for a trip to French Polynesia. He had bonded with the Polynesian islands and its people throughout his lifetime. Therefore, it was truly significant that the *Chieftain*, his pride and joy, should carry him to his most beloved destination.

From January until March of 1990, Carl Geringer and Alan Fleming prepared the ship for her maiden voyage through the South Pacific. Both Carl and Al had played an essential role in the construction of the *Chieftain*, and Baron chose them as his first two crewmembers, entrusting them with the task of forming a crew.

On April 1, 1990, the ship set sail with a crew of eleven people. A small group of close friends gathered at Pier 40 in Honolulu Harbor to wish Baron, the *Hawaiian Chieftain* and its crew *bon voyage*.

The *Hawaiian Chieftain's* departure for French Polynesia; Baron with
Gilligan at Pier 40 (Honolulu Harbor, April 1, 1990)

Baron was a skilled sailor despite having minimal experience. He had sailed in San Francisco Bay on his brother's classic yacht, a gorgeous 62-foot Sparksman & Stephens, handcrafted in 1937. Because he used to fly, he understood winds and wind direction. The *Chieftain* had over a hundred running lines and the crew needed to know the purpose of each one. While the ship was underway, Baron learned all of the lines and their functions. There was a lot to memorize, but with practice, it was like flying a plane. It came naturally to him.

The crew ate very well at sea. People who liked to cook assumed galley duty. Baron was never a chef, so he stayed out of the galley. The diverse menu included beef, chicken, pork, and an abundance of fresh-caught fish – everything from 10-pound mahi-mahi to 225-pound yellow fin tuna. The refrigerators were also stocked with an abundance of fresh fruits and vegetables.

In typical sailing tradition, when they crossed the equator, a celebratory rite of passage was held. Those who were crossing the equator for the first time were put through an initiation ritual. The sea was calm and the winds were light on that day in early April. Just prior to reaching zero latitude, the crew dropped the sails. Within moments, King Neptune, god of the sea, miraculously appeared on the ship! It was actually Baron dressed up in a white crown of shells and a long red beard made from shrimp peelings. A shell necklace was draped around his neck and he held a ten-foot trident in his hand.

Baron as King Neptune (writing on photo by Baron: April 1990, Tahiti bound
Hawaiian Chieftain stops at equator, 150 degrees west longitude)

King Neptune's job was to haze every crewmember that had never crossed the equator while under sail. Most members of the crew were "equator virgins". Those who were experienced became the King's assistants. One by one, the initiates were brought before the King and all kinds of garbage and food were thrown on them. Each novice was floured and egged and forced to tell jokes throughout the entire ordeal. Naturally, everyone was laughing hysterically, especially King Neptune! Once the initiates were completely humiliated and filthy, they were dunked in the ocean. One by one, each person was placed in the sling, plunged into the sea below, and baptized at the equator. By that point, it was a welcomed bath!

The ceremony took most of the afternoon and later everyone enjoyed the warm calm seas by swimming around the ship. That evening, a special meal was planned. Huge lobster tails were barbecued on the Weber grill on deck. Eventually, the sails were hoisted again, and the crew continued on their voyage to Tahiti. The trip was a dry voyage without alcohol, but on this special day, grog was served in measured quantities to celebrate the equator crossing.

The entire journey took twenty days and they arrived in Papeete on Friday, April 20, 1990. News had traveled quickly via the *coconut wireless*. People in Papeete eagerly awaited the arrival of Laurence Dorcy's tall ship – built and sailed from the Hawaiian Islands. As the *Chieftain* pulled into the harbor of Papeete, it was given a magnificent Tahitian welcome. Mr. Dorcy and the entire crew received leis and traditional Polynesian blessings. The local press was there to photograph and document the arrival, and the ship was moored at the Quay of Honor in the harbor of Papeete.

Baron playing honky-tonk music in a local restaurant
(Papeete, French Polynesia, April 1990)

Laurence and his crew stayed aboard the vessel for two weeks while it was docked in Papeete. Then they sailed it to the nearby island of Moorea with a French film crew on board. A portion of the two-hour sail was later broadcast on both Polynesian and French television stations.

The *Chieftain* anchored in Cook's Bay. When Baron set foot on the Island of Moorea, his local friends threw another reception for him. Mr. Dorcy had reserved a room at his favorite hotel, the Bali Hai at the head of Cook's Bay. This was the same hotel he regularly visited in the 1960s. He remained on the island for about two months, reconnecting with many of his island friends. Later, he flew back to California and another crew sailed the *Chieftain* to San Francisco. Having fulfilled his dream voyage to Tahiti, he decided to sell her and pursue new endeavors.

Hawaiian Chieftain anchored in Cook's Bay (Moorea, French Polynesia, May, 1990)

The Hawaiian Chieftain Today

Today, the *Hawaiian Chieftain* is based out of Grays Harbor Historical Seaport in Washington State. She sails up and down the west coast of North America, providing educational sailing programs that keep the history of tall ships alive for students in Kindergarten through Grade 12. Each year, the vessel that Laurence Dorcy commissioned and sailed to the South Pacific engages the young minds of over nine thousand youth.

Dorcy stayed in contact with Grays Harbor Historical Seaport Authority after they bought the *Chieftain*. He was invited aboard for her 10th anniversary sail on June 12, 1998, and attended her 20th anniversary party in Grays Harbor on June 12, 2008.

Baron aboard the *Hawaiian Chieftain* for her 10th anniversary sail (San Francisco Bay, June 12, 1998)

CHAPTER FIVE ~ LATER YEARS

California and Honolulu

In the mid 1990s, Dorcy bought a ranch style home in Los Altos, California, not far from his mother's home in Woodside. For Baron, the house's most important feature was the nine-car garage, which he filled with antique automobiles. The cars were in various stages of repair or disrepair, but for Baron, each one was a new project and a new story to tell. Besides his vehicular endeavors, he adopted a big dog, named Max, and some cats. He loved his pets and always arranged caretakers for them when he was away.

Baron's 1933 Duesenberg (California, 1996)

Laurence's love for the ocean and island life continued to entice him back to Hawaii. In the late 1990s, he bought two more condominiums at the Colony Surf as an investment and to accommodate visiting friends.

He continued to share his time between California and Hawaii. While staying in Waikiki, he would don a mask and snorkel almost every morning and swim in the warm waters of the Pacific Ocean. He loved wandering around the Honolulu flea market buying items made of beautiful shells and painted coral. He would take them apart and later, during his morning swims, he would scatter the shells and coral up and down the beach. This thoughtful endeavor was done to ensure that children and beachcombers had something pretty to find while exploring the beach.

Baron on the beach in front of the Colony Surf (Waikiki, 1998)

Maud's Final Days

Although Dorcy divided his time between his condo in Hawaii and his home in Los Altos, he frequently stayed with his mother near the end of her life. He had always been close to his mom, but in her later years, his presence was priceless to her.

With Maud's sharp memory beginning to fade, Laurence would tell her stories to remind her of the good old days. To keep his mother socially active, he often invited close friends for dinner.

Right until the end of her days, Maud refused to give up her car. Even after her license was revoked at age ninety-two, she continued to drive her car up and down the half-mile long driveway.

While Laurence was away at his condo in Hawaii, he received a phone call that his mother's health was declining. Immediately he flew back to California. Incidentally, Ann Pettigrew was on the same flight back to California, and they shared a conversation about his mother's failing health. But Laurence didn't know how serious the situation had become.

When he arrived at his mother's home, he realized the gravity of the situation, and quickly called Ann to join him. Laurence and Ann stayed at her bedside the entire night. Maud slipped away peacefully in her sleep the next morning. One of Maud's close friends said that Maud had waited for her son to be by her side, before she let herself pass on. She died at the age of ninety-four, in her own bed in her Woodside home on October 25, 1997.

A fond memory ~ Laurence sharing a special moment with his mother, Maud Hill,
after christening the *Hawaiian Chieftain* (Lahaina, Maui, June 12, 1988)

Kula Estate

Perhaps keenly aware of his own mortality after the passing of his mother, Laurence set his sights on a lasting legacy, a retirement home for himself. He began looking for a peaceful property on which to build his estate, one that would be akin to his mother's impressive homes and the noble dwellings of his ancestors, Louis and J.J. Hill.

In 1997, he discovered a 20-acre property in Kula, Maui, situated on the forested slopes of Haleakala at an elevation of 3200 feet. The lot had been used as a protea flower farm and vacation retreat, but was in disrepair. Nevertheless, Baron saw great potential for this impressive piece of land and decided to buy it. One of its finest features was the spectacular panoramic view of West Maui, the neighbor islands, and the expansive ocean horizon.

Baron's first mission was to construct a nine-bay garage for his antique cars. Next, the old house on the property was torn down and plans were laid for the mansion on the hill. The original caretaker's cottage was renovated and a two-story guesthouse was built at the front gate. The project started in 1998, and by 2005, the main house was complete. Improvements continued for another six years, but more and more, the estate reflected his prestigious background and artistic ingenuity.

Baron's 1953 Chevrolet truck in front of his nine-bay garage (Kula Estate, circa 2003)

To say the least, the property was beyond description. It was a mere twenty acres, compared to the hundreds of acres he enjoyed in his youth. But it was a work of art that emerged from a unique vision that reflected his fine taste and upbringing. Most importantly, it was something to make his family and friends proud.

Baron called it *Moemalie*, meaning place of peaceful rest. It was an exclusive Victorian-style gated manor, architecturally reminiscent of his mother's home in Woodside and the Mayfield Ranch. Elaborate manicured landscaping and lush terraced gardens surrounded the three-story residence, with nearly eight thousand square feet of living space and verandas. The three-acre front lawn was large enough to accommodate a helicopter landing.

The pool and poolside pavilion, complete with a billiards table and a stonewall fireplace, already existed on one of the terraces below the main house. However, Baron had the area freshly renovated and added a Big Green Egg ceramic barbecue and a cascading infinity pool. His friends surprised him by painting the image of a Maltese cross at the bottom of the pool during renovations. The symbol closely resembled the Maltese cross that he always wore around his neck.

The interior of the main house visually conveyed Laurence's rich family heritage. He often spoke of J.J. Hill and was grateful for the prosperity that was passed through the generations. In honor of his great grandfather, he commissioned a local Oahu artist to paint a large depiction of J.J. Hill from an old photograph. He hung it in the front foyer of his Maui estate. Antique red and green railroad lights were suspended high above the lobby. Baron always kept these lights illuminated to display the glistening reflection in the crystal chandelier and beveled glass windows.

Below the massive painting of J.J. Hill, Baron placed a framed newspaper clipping that featured his own claim-to-fame, the *Hawaiian Chieftain*. It was a 1995 *Los Angeles Times* article entitled "A Blast from the Past". The editorial contained a color photograph of the *Chieftain* firing a cannon in a mock battle against the *Pilgrim* schooner at the 10th annual Tall ships Festival in Dana Point, California.

Dorcy decorated the mansion with historical pictures and artifacts from his family lineage. The parlor and dining room were bursting with nostalgic images that spanned decades of family history, including pictures of his grandfathers, Louis W. Hill and Ben Holladay Dorcy, his father, Lt. Colonel Laurence Dorcy, and many depictions of his mother. A charming photograph of young Laurence, his sister, Sheilah, and their mom, taken at Pebble Beach, sat on a table in the parlor.

A large embroidered picture of his mother hung in the main hallway and he even kept her vintage Louis Vuitton traveling trunk on display. In one of the bedrooms, he placed an armoire that Maud had decoratively hand-painted for him as a child. She had inscribed his birth year across the top. This room also contained elaborately framed photographs of Laurence as a child. The dining chamber held a majestic table that transformed into an operational billiards board. His mother's family china and silver were kept in the adjacent credenza. In the loft suite, Laurence placed his wooden childhood table with three small chairs in the center of the room. His mother had kept it since his youth.

A custom-built elevator, designed to match the antique interior design, connected the three floors. The home conveyed a sense of old world elegance with four bedrooms, four full bathrooms, a large state-of-the-art kitchen, sitting rooms, a covered veranda and abundant open space. Vaulted ceilings, moldings, period windows and light fixtures, high quality finishes like Italian marble and exotic hardwood, all contributed to the ambiance of antiquity.

To add a unique flair, Baron hired an accomplished local artist, Karl Hensel, to paint imaginative and vibrant murals on many of the mansion walls. The seven pools of Hana, Maui, were painted cascading down the walls of the grand staircase. Framed artwork depicting famous Native American chiefs and warriors were also scattered on the walls over the main stairwell.

In Baron's octagonal bedroom, Karl Hensel crafted a sublime Egyptian theme, with majestic pyramids, pharaohs, hieroglyphs and columns. Exotic birds and plants surrounded an oasis of water and palm trees. Bedouins and camels walked across the desert sands. The entire octagonal ceiling above his bed was painted as a light blue sky and spotted with cottony white clouds. Baron asked the artist to paint a very meaningful image in the sky. It was a SAC aircraft in the process of refueling – attached by a flying boom to a smaller plane behind it.

On the main level, a gorgeous solarium with a large spa and lounge area was designed in nautical decor. Baron commissioned another local artist to create a stunning relief sculpture with various parts of the human form emerging from the white wall beside the hot tub. The artist took several casts of Baron's face and incorporated these into the artwork as well.

In line with his hobbies, Baron had a soundproof shooting range built deep under the three-car garage that was attached to the main house. Additionally, an enormous barn was constructed on the lower part of the property for servicing vehicles and maintaining his classic cars. It was well organized, with an up-to-date vehicle hoist, a machinist mill and lathe, a large loft for storage, and a small kitchen, bathroom and lounge area. One of Baron's friends, Bob Simpson, donated an array of antique garage memorabilia to decorate the walls. This included items such as vintage porcelain signs, collectible oilcans and antique license plates. This was a garage that most men only *dream* of having!

After the construction of the Kula estate was finished, Mr. Dorcy learned that a historical steam engine was ready for the scrap pile. It was located at the Kahuku Sugar Mill on the North Shore of Oahu. The mill opened in 1893 and was shut down in 1971. In the past, the steam engine had been used for processing sugar cane. Years later, it was displayed at the museum.

Baron bought this steam engine from the owner on Oahu and shipped it by barge to Maui. Then, the pieces of the old steam engine were trucked up the hill to Kula and laid out on the old tennis court of his property.

Over time, the steam engine was revitalized and reassembled by his friends, Dave Barrett, Dave Christophersen, George Tanji, Digger Lepard, and others. To make it run, a very large air compressor operated as a boiler. Once the steam engine was functional, he had a covered shelter with a shingled roof built around it.

Baron in front of his reconstructed steam engine (Kula Estate, 2007)

Dorcy heard that there were pieces of a larger steam engine at the Pu'unene Sugar Mill in Kahului, Maui. He acquired the pieces and had them hauled to his property. His intention was to rebuild the larger antique engine. However, this project was still in its infancy at the time of his passing.

Eventually, both steam engines were given to the Alexander & Baldwin Sugar Museum in Pu'unene in order to return them to public display. The Sugar Museum was one of the charitable beneficiaries named in Dorcy's will.

Laurence never lost sight that his fortune originated from J.J. Hill's Railroad Empire and in particular, that steam engines had played a major role in his prosperity. J.J.'s legacy was the motivation for rescuing these antique relics, which were headed for destruction. Baron kept these engines operational, so future generations could appreciate them.

Besides his construction projects, in 2003, Dorcy planted a ten-acre Koa tree farm on his property, with hopes of repopulating the vanishing native Hawaiian trees. His dream was to contribute large koa logs for traditional Hawaiian canoe carving. In order to make a canoe from a single log, a koa tree needs to grow vertically straight and be at least seventy-five years old. Therefore, the trees were specially groomed for this purpose. Specimens of this type are virtually nonexistent. Hopefully, years from now, trees planted on Dorcy's estate will be used for Hawaiian canoes. Again, he was showing remarkable vision for the future.

Baron beside his favorite and tallest tree in his Koa Forest (Kula Estate, 2008)

Father's Day Car Shows

Dorcy's friend, Johnny Baldwin, of the historic Baldwin missionary family in Maui, always hosted an annual Father's Day Car Show at his estate in Makawao. In 2005, they decided to hold it on Baron's sprawling front lawn at the Kula estate. Baron loved attending car shows in California and now he had the space to host his own car show! The invitation was extended to local car enthusiasts and approximately thirty cars showed up for the event. Car owners brought their family and friends and a potluck dish. A barbecue lunch was provided on the lawn and a band played all afternoon as Baron socialized and marveled over the magnificent antique cars.

Laurence Dorcy at a classic car show in California (date unknown)

Each year, the Father's Day Car Show grew in popularity. In total, Dorcy hosted five annual car shows, from 2005 to 2010. His close friends arranged the events, and Baron stayed on Maui for several days before and after the shows. By 2010, there were about seventy-five classic cars and hundreds of car aficionados mingling and enjoying an afternoon picnic on Baron's picturesque property. Annually, he would fire up the rebuilt steam engine and show the guests how it worked.

Baron always welcomed the striking array of classic cars that were neatly dispersed across his luscious green lawn. He would ride around in one of his golf carts and examine each one. He felt a sense of pride in displaying his own car collection. But most of all, he loved to talk story with like-minded people who shared his life-long passion for these unique and timeless classics.

Baron at his annual Father's Day Car Show (Kula Estate, June, 2007)

One of Dorcy's exceptional cars was a classic 1916 American LaFrance Speedster. It was originally a fire truck that was converted into a road racer. In its day, it was a powerful fast car. It had a massive 855 cubic inch engine with three spark plugs per cylinder, a twin sprocket chain drive, a four-inch open exhaust and wooden spoke wheels. It weighed 6200 pounds and averaged only one mile per gallon of gasoline. To personalize this extraordinary vehicle, Laurence had the Dorcy family emblem painted on the fuel tank.

Baron's 1916 American LaFrance at the Kula Estate; insert at top right is a custom hand-painted
Dorcy family emblem on the fuel tank (Kula Estate, June, 2010)

Get Your Motor Running...

Laurence's passion for classic cars lived with him from childhood until the last days of his life. A close friend recalled a very special journey with him in California. Baron had to drive from Palo Alto to San Carlos, drop off a car, and pick up a bright red convertible. She joined him for the drive there and back. When they got on the Bay Shore Freeway, he took off like a teenager. It was pedal to the medal!

He sped down the freeway with the top down and his ponytail flying in the wind, passing cars and weaving in and out of traffic. With a huge smile on his face, he told his friend that he was glad she was there, because no one else would let him drive like that! She recalled the story with a chuckle, "I wondered what I had gotten myself into! But I said a few prayers and we got home safe, without any fender benders or worse! He really *loved* his cars!"

Baron in his 1950s model corvette at Hileman Automotive Service
(Palo Alto, California, circa 1990)

Return to his Roots

One of Baron's life-long desires was to see his great grandfather's steam locomotive, the *William Crooks*, at the Lake Superior Railroad Museum in Duluth. In the fall of 2010, Ann Pettigrew joined him on a trip to Saint Paul, Minnesota. His cousin, Bill Ferguson, greeted them at the airport and drove them to Duluth. The museum staff was so pleased by his visit. They honored the great grandson of J.J. Hill by arranging a special train ride and luncheon for him on a Great Northern Railway private car. They made the entire day a tribute to Laurence Holmes Dorcy Jr., the great grandson of J.J. Hill. It was a very meaningful trip for Baron (see photo front cover).

On the way back to Saint Paul, they stopped at J.J. Hill's family farm, in North Oaks, where Baron's family used to vacation in the summer. The house is now an open-air museum that preserves the buildings of J.J.'s 3300-acre farm. Laurence also toured the house where his mother grew up. At the age of seventy-five, returning to his family roots and visiting places he had been as a child elicited many fond memories. Sadly, he passed on less than a year after this evocative trip.

CHAPTER SIX ~ REMEMBERING BARON

Celebration of Life

On June 2, 2011, Laurence H. Dorcy Jr. died of respiratory failure at Straub Hospital in Honolulu. Violent thunderstorms hit Honolulu that evening while those who loved him grieved the loss of their dear friend.

A few weeks later, Grays Harbor Historical Seaport Authority remembered and honored Laurence H. Dorcy aboard the *Hawaiian Chieftain*. They tossed a lei into the sea from the quarterdeck, dipped the flag and gave him a 13-gun salute. Baron definitely would have been pleased.

A year later, on June 16, 2012, a celebration of life was held at Baron's Kula estate. It was attended by dozens of his closest friends, who joined together to remember his adventurous life. The following day, Baron's trademark Father's Day Car Show was held for the last time on the Kula property. This time it was held in honor and remembrance of Laurence 'The Baron' Dorcy.

A record crowd attended the event. They reminisced about the days when he had hosted the car shows and shared their favorite Baron stories. Since 2005, he had brought hundreds of car enthusiasts together to talk story and share an incredible day at his picturesque estate. To celebrate this achievement, over seventy cars spread across his front lawn for a final farewell.

Father's Day Memorial Car Show in memory of Laurence H. Dorcy Jr. (Kula Estate, 2012)

Baron Returns to the Sea

With Baron's celebration of life complete in Hawaii, it was time for an ultimate departure – the spreading of his ashes. Throughout his life, Baron often spoke of his love for French Polynesia and its people. Obviously this place had made quite an impression on him. His final wish, as stated in his last will and testament, was to have his friend, Carl Geringer, scatter his ashes in Cook's Bay, off the island of Moorea. This is where his tall ship, the *Hawaiian Chieftain*, had anchored more than 20 years earlier.

In the summer of 2012, Carl contacted Patricia Lee, the Honorary French Consul in Honolulu, who worked diligently with the San Francisco French Consulate to secure all the permissions. They worked together to complete the vast amount of paperwork necessary to transport Baron's ashes to French Polynesia. Normally arrangements need to be made directly through the San Francisco Consulate. But the Honolulu office staff simplified the process, so Carl did not have to travel to San Francisco.

Once the initial paperwork was complete, Carl contacted the Mayor of Moorea and was granted tentative authorization to scatter the ashes in Cook's Bay. Without the help of the offices in Honolulu and San Francisco, as well as Baron's notoriety on Moorea, it would have been a much more daunting task. Besides the mountain of paperwork, it was difficult to obtain permission because cremation does not exist in French Polynesia. In the past, royalty and high-ranking Polynesians were buried in caverns on the side of mountainous cliffs. The exact location was concealed to protect the sanctity of the tombs. Today, simple burial is the custom in French Polynesian society. Since ash scattering is foreign to their culture, Mr. Geringer remains grateful to the French Polynesian diplomats for their support. Just days before he left for Tahiti, the Honolulu office wrapped Baron's urn in ribbon made with the French flag colors, sealed it with hot wax, and stamped it with the official signet of the Consulate.

Carl carefully packed the urn in Baron's satchel, the same bag that Baron had always carried with his books and photo albums. Ready to carry out Baron's final wishes, Carl and a small group of Baron's friends flew to Tahiti on September 15, 2012. When the group arrived at the Papeete airport, the scene was reminiscent of the *Hawaiian Chieftain's* first arrival in Papeete harbor. More than a dozen friends greeted them with traditional Polynesian leis and flower headbands. The greeting committee was full of aloha spirit, yet saddened by the loss of their friend.

The following day, the group traveled by ferry to Moorea, as Baron had done many times before. They stayed at the Hugh Kelley family beach house near the entrance to Cook's Bay. Hugh was one of the Bali Hai boys who had established the Bali Hai Hotel on Moorea. The beach house still remains next door to the former hotel, which was sold and turned into the Moorea Pearl Resort.

The group anxiously awaited the Mayor's final stamp of approval for the ceremony, but it took another three business days and many trips to the Municipal office to get consent. The sky was overcast and the wind and seas were turbulent while they awaited authorization. Due to strong winds, it was unsafe to take a boat through Cook's Bay. But when the Mayor personally gave his endorsement, the weather, wind and seas suddenly calmed, and the ceremony was scheduled for the following day, September 20, 2012.

With permission in hand, they quickly finalized their plans. Tahitian and American friends worked side by side for hours on beautiful flower leis, headbands, and decorations for Baron's final journey by boat. Tiri Hoffsten, who worked on the Maui estate and was the son of Baron's close friend on Moorea, Texas Bob, organized a 30-foot boat with a traditional Polynesian thatched roof. The group nicknamed it the *Leaky Tiki* after the name of a real boat, the *Liki Tiki* that Baron used to take between the Club Bali Hai and the Hotel Bali Hai years earlier.

His final farewell ceremony aboard the *Leaky Tiki* may have been a far cry from his first luxury cruise across the Atlantic on the *Normandie*, at age two. But those who knew Baron understood that he would be just as comfortable on a modest Polynesian boat, as he was on a luxury cruise ship.

The boat left the dock by the old Hotel Bali Hai at 3:30 pm. After a few minutes, Mako, the Tahitian owner and captain, stopped the engine. He blessed everyone aboard with a traditional Polynesian chant. Then he asked permission from the gods to allow them to respectfully step off the land, and enter the ocean's domain on their mission to say goodbye to Baron. After a short pause, they continued their journey to the heart of Cook's Bay.

Local musicians had volunteered their services to be part of the *Ohana,* or family. They played awe-inspiring music on their traditional instruments. There was nothing but the sound of two voices singing, a guitar and a ukulele. It was like a journey back in time – a spiritual ceremony that honored the traditions of the Polynesians and the wishes of their dear friend Baron.

They motored the boat to the exact spot where Baron had anchored the *Hawaiian Chieftain* more than twenty years earlier. Carl Geringer was the only one aboard who had been on the *Chieftain's* maiden voyage with Baron. He recalled the final passage as "a peaceful and serene voyage, with Baron guiding us through the Tahitian spirits and touching all of us in a way that cannot be described."

While the *Leaky Tiki* drifted in the heart of Cook's Bay, Mako delivered the service in Tahitian. Al Bento, a reverend and fisherman from Honolulu, conducted the service in English and Hawaiian. As Carl scattered Baron's remains into the deep waters of the bay, there was a sense of calm resolve. Baron's wishes had been honored. He had returned to the warm seas of French Polynesia – a place he held dear to his heart. Reverend Al expressed the significance of scattering ashes at sea. He said that "when someone's ashes are scattered at sea, no matter where we are in the world – when we swim in the ocean, that person is touching us, and we are touching them."

Baron Swimming at the equator
Hawaiian Chieftain's maiden voyage to Tahiti (April, 1990)

At the end of this rite of passage, Baron's friends tossed leis and flowers into the water and drank Tahitian Hinano beer in his honor. They poured some Hinano into Cook's Bay for their departed friend and said their final goodbyes. As people shared stories of Baron, there was an overwhelming sense of gratitude for his presence in their lives.

During the return trip to the dock, the musicians played pleasant Tahitian music that Baron had loved so much during his lifetime. Everyone felt a sense of satisfaction in the beauty and tranquility of the service. It was everything Baron would have wanted, and more. It was traditional, low key, and involved friends from both America and Tahiti.

Throughout his lifetime, Laurence Holmes Dorcy Jr. had traveled on luxury cruise lines, private railcars, flown aircraft in the Air Force, built and sailed a tall ship to Tahiti, and driven numerous antique cars. But his final mode of transportation was the wind and sea. He had chosen his final resting place, and with the help of his friends, he had returned. As they say in Tahitian: *Tei iā 'oe na te hau.* Peace be with you, Baron.

Leis and flowers in Cook's Bay after scattering Baron's ashes (Moorea, French Polynesia, 2012)

REFERENCES

Interviewees and Contributors (alphabetically)

Dave Barrett (Kihei, Hawaii)
Al Bento (Honolulu, Hawaii)
Linda Burns (Santa Monica, California)
Jay Carlisle (Moorea, French Polynesia)
Clinton Churchill (Honolulu and Kula, Hawaii)
Kila DeMello (Captain Cook, Hawaii)
Daryl B. Dorcy (Libertyville, Illinois)
Andreas Drenters (Rockwood, Ontario, Canada)
Nicklos Dudley (Honolulu, Hawaii)
Carl Geringer (Honolulu, Hawaii)
Isaac Hall (Wailuku, Maui)
Greg Hardie (Moorea, French Polynesia)
Alexandre Tiri Hoffsten (Kula, Hawaii)
Elsa Firiapu Hoffsten (Kula, Hawaii)
Jeanne Hoffsten (Moorea, French Polynesia)
John Hogan (Moorea, French Polynesia)
Linda Ipsen (Honolulu, Hawaii)
Beryl McDougall (Rockwood, Ontario, Canada)
John McManus (Sausalito, California)
Jeff Peterson (North Oaks, Minnesota)
Ann Pettigrew (San Francisco, California)
Bob Simpson (Hawaii)
Dallas Tauiari'i Cowan (Papeete, French Polynesia)
Jack Haven Ward (Honolulu, Hawaii)
Linda West (Honolulu, Hawaii)
Teva Wilkes (Moorea, French Polynesia)
Drew Womack (Hawaii)

Newspapers and Journals

[1] "Worry Kills; Work Kills Worry: Motto of America's Oldest Engineer". *Tacoma Times*. September 6, 1909. p. 6. Retrieved via Newspapers.com.

"A Blast from the Past." *Los Angeles Times* 10 Sept. 1995. Print.

"An Interesting Wedding Ending a Pretty Romance." *The Oregonian* [Portland] 18 June 1899. Web.

"B-25 With Hydraulic Failure Landed by Students." *Roundup,* Vol. VIII, No. 51 8 Nov. 1957. Print.

"Heiress to Hill Fortune Marries California Writer." *The Salt Lake Tribune* 17 Mar. 1933: 3. Web.

"Heir to Hill Railroad Millions Weds Writer." *The Ironwood Daily Globe* 17 Mar. 1933. Web.

"Heir to Millions Marries." *The Daily Northwestern* [Evanston] 17 Mar. 1933. Web.

"Hill Heiress and S.F. Man to Wed." *The Oakland Tribune* 15 Mar. 1933. Web.

"Hill Kin Weds Coast Writer: Daughter of St. Paul Woman is to Honey-moon in Honolulu." *The Billings Gazette* 17 Mar. 1933. Web.

"Maud Dorcy To Marry Austrian Ski Champ." *The News-Palladium* [Benton Harbor] 24 July 1943. Web.

"Maud Hill Wed to Californian: Nuptials for Daughter of Louis Hill of St. Paul at Del Monte." *The Mason City Globe-Gazette* 16 Mar. 1933. Web.

"Milestones: Married." *Time: The Weekly Newsmagazine* Vol. XXI No. 13 [Chicago] 27 Mar. 1933: 32. Print.

"Wed at Del Monte." *Berkeley Daily Gazette* 17 Mar. 1933: 5. Web.

Books and Websites

"50 Olu Olu Place | Kula, Maui | Ultimate Serenity." *YouTube*. YouTube, Web.

"Albert Schweitzer." *IMDb*. IMDb.com. Web.

"Alexander & Baldwin Sugar Museum." *Alexander & Baldwin Sugar Museum*. Web.

"Genealogy, Family Trees & Family History Records at Ancestry.com." *Genealogy, Family Trees & Family History Records at Ancestry.com*. Web.

"Hawaiian Chieftain." *Grays Harbor Historical Seaport Authority*. Web.

Hensel, Karl. *Karlhensel.com*. (Aquarium Panels, Egyptian Style, Egyptian Additions, Grand Staircase, Rose Trellis, Peacock Archway, Seven Pools) Web.

Hickman, Kennedy. "*USS Enterprise CV-6 World War II Aircraft Carrier*." Web.

"Hill Farm Historical Society." *Hill Farm Historical Society*. Web.

Hill, Mary T. Diary, 1903. *Minnesota Historical Society*. Web.

"Kahuku Sugar Mill - Shaka Sign History - North Shore, Oahu Hawaii." *Kahukusugarmill*. Web.

"Lake Superior Railroad Museum." *Train Excursions*. Web.

Malone, Michael P. *James J. Hill: Empire Builder of the Northwest*. Norman: U of Oklahoma, 1996. Print.

Matthews, John. *Complete American Armoury and Blue Book*. Genealogical Publishing Company, 2009. Web.

"Minnesota Historical Society." *Minnesota Historical Society*. Web.

"Naval History and Heritage Command." *Enterprise VII (CV-6)*. Web.

"Newspaper Abstracts: Main." *Newspaper Abstracts*. Web.

"Railroad Baron Edward Harriman is Born." *History.com*. A&E Television Networks. Web.

Stanford Alumni Directory, 1992, p. 330.

"The USS Enterprise CV 6 – Heroes, History, Honor and More." *The USS Enterprise CV 6 Heroes History Honor*. Web.

"Tiki Bar & Restaurant." *La Mariana Sailing Club*. Web.

"USS Enterprise CV-6 The Most Decorated Ship of the Second World War." *USS Enterprise CV-6*. Web.

Laurence H. Dorcy Jr., also known as "Baron", was the great grandson of railroad magnate, James Jerome Hill. Born into a world of privilege in 1935, Baron became heir to a substantial fortune. This color photo biography illustrates some of this gifted man's exciting endeavors, such as the construction of the *Hawaiian Chieftain,* a tall ship that continues to educate youth on the Pacific coast of America. This book describes Baron's rich family ancestry, his childhood during WWII, his Air Force duty in Strategic Air Command in the 1950s, his beach days in French Polynesia in the 60s, explorations between California, Hawaii and the French Polynesian islands, the *Hawaiian Chieftain's* maiden voyage to Tahiti, and the breathtaking creation of his final estate in Maui. After his passing in 2011, the formation of the Laurence H. Dorcy Hawaiian Foundation, which generously supports charities in Hawaii, ensures that his legacy lives on.

Kathy Lynne Linker has published several stories in the best-selling trade paperback series of all time, *Chicken Soup for the Soul.* She has avidly traveled the world, seeking new experiences and adventures in over forty countries. Chilly childhood winters in Ontario, Canada pushed her to seek the warm beaches of Hawaii and French Polynesia, where she loves to sail and snorkel. She considers Italy her second home since she has traveled and lived there on many occasions. On her journeys abroad, she loves to speak French, Italian and Spanish, eat local cuisine and immerse herself in local arts, music and culture. With a BA in Psychology and a Masters degree in Education, she has been teaching, researching and writing around the globe. (Photo: Kathy in the rumble seat of Baron's 1931 Ford Model A, Kula Estate, Maui, 2014)

Printed in the United States
By Bookmasters